Microlife

Scientists and Discoveries

Robert Snedden

Heinemann
LIBRARY

First published in Great Britain by Heinemann Library,
Halley Court, Jordan Hill, Oxford OX2 8EJ,
a division of Reed Educational and Professional Publishing Ltd.
Heinemann is a registered trademark of Reed Educational & Professional Publishing Limited.

OXFORD MELBOURNE AUCKLAND
JOHANNESBURG BLANTYRE GABORONE
IBADAN PORTSMOUTH NH (USA) CHICAGO

Produced by Paul Davies and Associates
Originated by Ambassador Litho Ltd
Printed in Hong Kong/China

04 03 02 01 00
10 9 8 7 6 5 4 3 2 1

ISBN 0 431 09276 1

British Library Cataloguing in Publication Data

Sneeden, Robert
Scientists and discoveries. – (Microlife)
1. Discoveries in science – Juvenile literature 2. Medicine – Juvenile literature 3. Inventions – Juvenile literature
I. Title
509

ISBN 0431092761

Acknowledgements
The Publishers would like to thank the following for permission to reproduce photographs:
Image Select: Ann Ronan Picture Library pp4, 8, 9, 10, 11, 12, 15, 16, 24, 25, 27, 32; Science Photo Library: pp28, 34, 39, A Barrington Brown p43, J Berger, Max-Planck Institute p29, Dr J Burgess pp17, 20, 22, 35, EM Unit, VLA p45 J King-Holmes/OCMS pp36, 41, J Lewin, EM Unit, Royal Free Hospital p31, R Maisonneuve, Publiphoto Diffusion pp7, 19, Dr G Murti p14, NIBSC p23, C Priest & M Clarke p13, H Raguet/Eurelios p44; Telegraph Colour Library: M Simpson p21, A Traza p5.

Cover photograph reproduced with permission of CNRI, Science Photo Library.

The Publishers would like to thank Dr Puran Ganeri for his comments in the preparation of this title.

Every effort has been made to contact copyright holders of any material reproduced in this book. Any omissions will be rectified in subsequent printings if notice is given to the Publisher.

For more information about Heinemann Library books, or to order, please phone ++44 (0)1865 888066, or send a fax to ++44 (0)1865 314091. You can visit our website at www.heinemann.co.uk.

Any words appearing in the text in bold, **like this**, are explained in the Glossary.

CONTENTS

INTRODUCTION

In 1674 a Dutch businessman who had no formal scientific training took a sample of water from a lake near his home in Delft and examined it through a microscope that he had made himself. As he did so, Antonie van Leeuwenhoek took the first glimpse into the invisible kingdoms of the living world.

A cartoon of Louis Pasteur, published in 1887. He used rabbits in his research into rabies. Debate still rages over whether animals should be used in medical research.

Leeuwenhoek, along with other early explorers of the unseen kingdoms of life, such as Robert Hooke, began to reveal information about a previously unknown and unsuspected world of microscopic life forms. At first, people could scarcely believe that such life forms existed, but during the past 300 years many scientists have worked hard to piece together a picture of the microscopic world and the way in which it relates to our larger world.

GERM THEORY

In 1835 Agostino Bassi (1773–1856), an Italian scientist, showed that a disease affecting silkworms was caused by a **fungus**. This was the first time that a **micro-organism** was recognized as an agent of animal disease. Bassi was also the first to suggest that some infectious diseases suffered by humans are also caused by microscopic **parasites**. Just over 20 years later, in 1857, Louis Pasteur proposed his 'germ theory' of disease, showing that for every infectious illness there is a micro-organism that is the cause of it.

Ten years later Joseph Lister revolutionized surgery when he introduced **antiseptics** into the operating theatre to hold at bay the infective **bacteria** that had claimed so many lives. By simply spraying carbolic acid on surgical instruments, wounds and dressings, he dramatically reduced the number of deaths due to bacterial infection after surgery.

UNRAVELLING LIFE'S SECRETS

German **bacteriologist** Robert Koch developed Pasteur's germ theory and published 'Koch's Postulates' in 1884, a series of tests to determine the involvement of a micro-organism in a disease. The tests are still largely practised today.

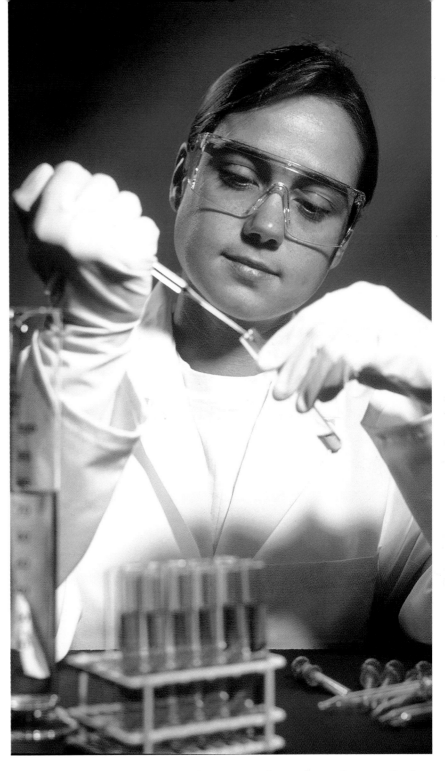

A modern-day medical researcher measures solutions using equipment that Pasteur would have recognized.

In the last 100 years our knowledge of the microscopic secrets of life has increased dramatically. We have unravelled the **genetic** code, the set of instructions for building a new organism passed on from generation to generation. Yet life can still surprise us – as it has with the recent discovery of the **prion**, a previously unknown form of disease agent.

THE JANSENS AND THE COMPOUND MICROSCOPE

The idea of using lenses to improve vision has been around for a long time. Stories are told of the Roman Emperor Nero watching events in the arena magnified through an emerald.

The English thinker Roger Bacon (c.1220–92) is sometimes credited with the invention of spectacles, but it is likely that several people came up with the idea in different places and at different times. After the invention of spectacles it was only a matter of time before someone put two lenses in front of each other and discovered that they had made the first compound microscope. ('Compound' simply means that it uses two or more lenses.)

NEAR OR FAR?

There is some question as to which came first, the telescope, to see far away, or the microscope, to see up-close. Since a microscope uses lenses in a similar way to a telescope, one idea may have led to the other. It seems certain, however, that the late-16th and early-17th century lens-makers of Holland were involved with these inventions.

THE JANSENS

Credit for inventing the first microscope is usually given to Zacharias Jansen, who supposedly made a simple instrument, consisting of two lenses mounted in a sliding tube, in around 1600. It is possible that his father, Hans, actually made the first one. Unfortunately no early Jansen microscope has survived and there are no clear details of their construction.

THE ROYAL MICROSCOPES

According to the custom of the time, the Jansens made several versions of their new invention as gifts for Prince Maurice of Orange and Archduke Albert of Austria. The royal instruments were described as being composed of three sliding tubes, 46 centimetres long when fully extended, and just under

1 centimetre in diameter. They were very ornate, with three brass dolphins at the end forming the feet of a tripod.

MICROSCOPY MOVES ON

The Jansen microscopes were not particularly powerful. They were said to have a magnification of three times when fully closed and nine times when fully extended. Today a good hand lens, magnifying ten times or more, would produce better results. However, word of the new invention spread rapidly and within just a few years many microscope makers appeared throughout Europe. It could be said that the first major improvement in microscope **optics** was the introduction of a three-lens system, the inventor of which may well have been the English scientist Robert Hooke. The exploration of the micro-world could now begin.

Microscopes have developed a long way since the pioneering work of the Jansens. This electron microscope is 100 times more powerful than the most-advanced microscope using lenses.

ROBERT HOOKE AND HIS SMALL DRAWINGS

Robert Hooke (1635–1703) has been described as the greatest experimental scientist of the 17th century. His interests ranged from physics and astronomy to chemistry, biology and geology. He worked with the great architect Sir Christopher Wren and helped rebuild London after the Great Fire of 1666. He assisted the physicist Robert Boyle in working out the physics of gases and corresponded with many other eminent scientists of his day. Hooke made major contributions in many fields of science, including biology.

THE INVISIBLE EXPERT

Surprisingly for such an eminent scientist, no portraits of Robert Hooke have ever been identified.

MICROGRAPHIA

Hooke's fame as a biologist largely comes from one book. In 1665 he published *Micrographia* (the title means small drawings). It was perhaps the first book to reveal the huge potential of the microscope to open up the living world. In it he detailed the observations he had made with a microscope. He examined bird feathers, insects, sponges and other natural objects. His observations were highly detailed and accurate and he made marvellous drawings of the things that he saw.

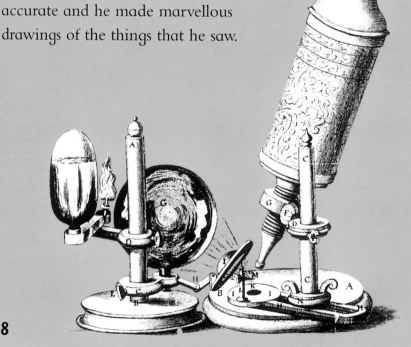

One of Robert Hooke's microscopes. A glass globe filled with water was used to concentrate light on the object being examined.

8

THE DISCOVERY OF THE CELL

One of Hooke's best known observations was his study of thin slices of cork. He wrote, 'I could exceedingly plainly perceive it to be all perforated and porous. ... These pores, or **cells**, ... were indeed the first microscopical pores I ever saw, and perhaps, that were ever seen.'

This was the first time that the word 'cell' was used in its biological sense of a unit of life. The word comes from the Latin *cellula*, meaning a small room. What Hooke saw were the dead walls of formerly living cells. Hooke had discovered plant cells, although at the time he had no notion that this was what they were.

Hooke was the first person to examine fossils with a microscope. He saw that there were close similarities between the structures of petrified wood and fossil shells and living wood and living shells.

Hooke made many improvements to the compound microscope and produced one of the finest microscopes of his time. *Micrographia* gives details of the microscopes he used. Hooke thought that a single-lens microscope would probably give the best results but that this would be difficult to use. He was right, and in just a few years a Dutch draper from Delft would be producing stunning results using just such a microscope.

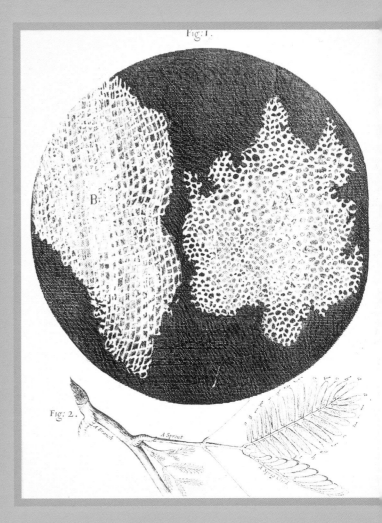

Robert Hooke's drawing of the cells he saw in a thin slice of cork.

ANTONIE VAN LEEUWENHOEK AND HIS LITTLE ANIMALS

Antonie van Leeuwenhoek (1632–1723) came from a family of tradesmen. Leeuwenhoek earned his living as a draper. He had no higher education, but with skill, patience and a boundless curiosity he succeeded in making some of the most important discoveries in the history of biology.

THE SINGLE LENS MICROSCOPE

At some point before 1668, Leeuwenhoek learned to grind glass to make lenses and construct simple microscopes. He seems to have been inspired by Robert Hooke's popular book *Micrographia*, which detailed Hooke's own discoveries with a microscope. Leeuwenhoek's microscopes were basically powerful magnifying glasses rather than compound microscopes of the type used by Hooke and today's scientists.

Compared to a modern microscope, Leeuwenhoek's microscope was a simple device. The entire instrument was only about 10 centimetres long. It had a single lens, which was mounted in a tiny hole in a brass plate. The specimen to be observed was placed on a sharp point set in front of the lens. The point could be adjusted by turning two screws. The microscope had to be held close to the eye and needed good lighting. In all, Leeuwenhoek is known to have made over 500 of his microscopes. Fewer than ten of them have survived.

One of Leeuwenhoek's brass microscopes.

A CAREFUL OBSERVER

Leeuwenhoek showed great skill at grinding lenses. His microscopes magnified over 200 times, and produced clearer and brighter images than any that could be achieved using the compound microscopes of the time. He was also a diligent observer and took great care in describing what he saw. He hired an illustrator to prepare drawings of the things he saw because he could not draw well himself.

BACTERIA REVEALED

In 1673, Leeuwenhoek began writing letters to the newly formed Royal Society of London, describing what he had seen with his microscopes. For the next 50 years he corresponded with the Royal Society, describing the wonders his microscopes revealed, including descriptions of many **protists**, which he referred to as 'little animals'.

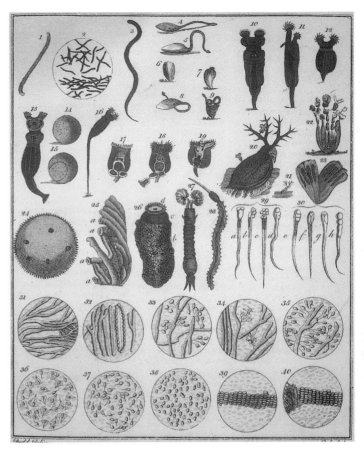

A few of the many wonders of the microscopic world seen for the first time by Leeuwenhoek.

On 17 September 1683, Leeuwenhoek wrote to the Royal Society regarding observations on the plaque between his own teeth and on those of two old men who had never cleaned their teeth. Leeuwenhoek reported how in his own mouth he saw 'many very little, living animalcules, very prettily a-moving'. In the mouth of one of the old men, he found 'an unbelievably great company of living animalcules … The biggest … bent their body into curves in going forwards … the other animalcules were in such enormous numbers, that all the water … seemed to be alive.' These were perhaps the first descriptions of **bacteria** ever recorded.

Leeuwenhoek also discovered blood **cells**, and was the first to see living sperm cells of animals. He observed free-living and **parasitic** microscopic protists, microscopic nematode worms and much more. He continued his observations until the last days of his life.

EDWARD JENNER AND VACCINATION

For at least 1000 years people have known that exposure to a disease agent can give protection against later encounters with the disease as the body develops an immunity to it. The procedure of introducing a substance into the body to give immunity is called inoculation.

SCAB SNIFFING

As early as AD900 the Chinese had a secret method of fending off smallpox. It involved grinding up pox scabs and inhaling them. It seems to have worked, although there was always the risk that the person would develop a full-blown and possibly fatal dose of the disease.

VARIOLATION

A cartoon of the time that made fun of Jenner's idea of injecting people with cowpox.

A version of the Chinese practice was eventually brought to Britain in 1717 by Lady Mary Wortley Montagu. Small amounts of fluid from smallpox blisters were administered to people in a process known as variolation. Usually, inoculated individuals experienced only a mild form of the disease. Some, however, became severely ill and died.

THE FIRST VACCINATION

In 1796 Edward Jenner, a country doctor, discovered that he could safely give immunity against smallpox by inoculating patients with fluid from cowpox blisters. The cowpox **virus** is similar to the smallpox virus but is a mild disease that humans sometimes catch from cows. Jenner took some fluid from blisters on the hand of a milkmaid who had cowpox and then injected it into eight-year-old James Phipps. Not unexpectedly, James contracted cowpox. After waiting for two months, Jenner then inoculated James with fluid from the blisters of a person with smallpox. James did not contract smallpox. Two years later, Jenner successfully repeated the experiment and published his findings.

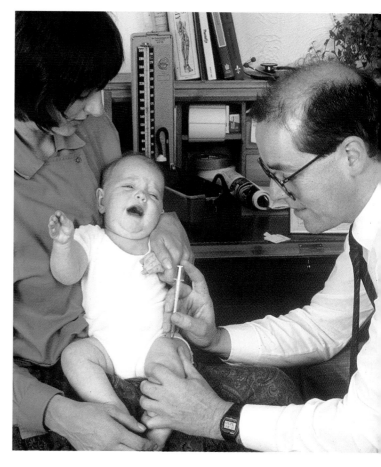

Vaccinations are now an everyday part of the fight against infectious diseases.

A JUSTIFIED RISK

Jenner's actions in putting the boy's life at risk would never get passed by any **ethics** committee today. However, his success led to the rapid acceptance and application of the procedure, which later came to be called **vaccination**, across Europe and other parts of the world. His work was a first step on the path to the development of vaccines against other infectious diseases as well. In the following century Louis Pasteur demonstrated that weakened disease agents could be used to give immunity to other diseases. As for smallpox, because of a global campaign by the World Health Organization, the disease was declared to have been completely eradicated from the planet by 1977.

Schleiden, Schwann and the Theory of Cells

Matthias Jakob Schleiden (1804–81) was educated in law but he was much more fascinated by the world of plants. The study of botany became more than a hobby for him and, in 1831, he began to study botany and medicine at universities in Göttingen and Berlin. In 1838 Schleiden began a series of careful studies of different types of plant tissue under the microscope. What he saw led him to propose that all plants are made of **cells**. Schleiden said that the cell is the basic unit of all plants and the growth of a plant consists of the production and development of new cells.

A section through a mammal cell, stained to show up different structures. The cell nucleus is shown in pink.

Cell Theory

The German **physiologist** Theodor Schwann (1810–82) extended the theory to include all living things. Schwann had studied medicine at the University of Berlin and had made a detailed microscopic study of animal tissue, just as Schleiden had done for plants. This led to his idea that all living things are made up of cells and that each cell has certain essential features, such as a **nucleus**. Both men made an equal contribution to our knowledge of the structure of living things and they are given equal credit for developing the cell theory. The theory soon drew the attention of other biologists to the study of the contents of the cell.

SINGLE-CELLED ORGANISMS

The discovery of the importance of the cell was one of the most significant in the history of biology. In 1845 Karl Siebold (1804–85), a German zoologist, published a book about the microscopically small **protists** that had been discovered 200 years earlier by Leeuwenhoek. He showed that these organisms were single-celled. Life, it seemed, could be composed of just one cell. As we now know, there are, in fact, many more single-celled life forms than there are larger multi-celled forms such as ourselves.

'ALL CELLS ARISE FROM CELLS'

Rudolf Carl Virchow (1821–1902) further advanced the cell theory when he established a fundamental principle of biology that 'all cells arise from cells'. He also carried out research into cell function in disease, showing that the cells of diseased tissue are descended from the cells of healthy tissue. He was the first to bring the study of disease down to the level of the cell. He saw disease as being rather like a war between cells in the body. Louis Pasteur would show that disease could be caused by a number of outside agents.

A portrait of Theodor Schwann, one of the founders of the study of cells.

LOUIS PASTEUR AND THE GERM THEORY

Louis Pasteur (1822–95) set one of the foundation stones of the science of microbiology. His germ theory of disease (the idea that most infectious diseases are caused by germs) is one of the most important developments in medical history.

Louis Pasteur, one of the greatest of all scientists, shown here in later life.

A LIFE IN SCIENCE

Pasteur was born in Dole, in the Jura region of France. He received his scientific education at the Ecole Normale Supérieure in Paris, obtaining his doctorate in 1847. He taught for the next few years as a professor of science in Dijon and Strasbourg, then as Professor of Chemistry and Dean of the Lille **Faculty** of Sciences. In 1857 he returned to the Ecole Normale as Dean of Sciences until 1867, when he was appointed Professor of Chemistry at the Sorbonne. In 1888 he became the founder and director of the Pasteur Institute.

THE GERM OF AN IDEA

At the request of a distiller from the north of France, Pasteur began to examine why alcohol becomes contaminated with undesirable substances during **fermentation**. The theory of fermentation in favour at that time was that yeast acts as a chemical **catalyst** in the process. Pasteur guessed that yeast is not a chemical but a microscopic organism, and that the conversion of sugar into alcohol is caused by the biological activity of the yeast.

He also guessed that the undesirable substances in the wine were being produced by other **micro-organisms** present in the mix. One type of micro-organism, which he called the germ, acted on one type of substance to produce another substance.

Pasteur was able to illustrate his theory with a series of experiments that involved converting sugar into lactic acid or into alcohol, alcohol into acetic acid and so forth, all brought about by micro-organisms.

'ON LACTIC FERMENTATION'

His germ theory of fermentation was first presented in 1857 in a classic short paper, *'Sur la fermentation appelée lactique'* ('On lactic fermentation'). In this Pasteur claimed that the different types of microbes could be separated from each other by proper techniques, and their different properties examined. He suggested that, just as each type of fermentation is caused by a particular type of germ, so too are many types of disease.

LIFE WITHOUT AIR

Another of Pasteur's great achievements in the field of **biochemistry** was his discovery that some micro-organisms do not need oxygen to survive. Most living things, including us, get energy from a series of reactions that make use of oxygen. This is called respiration. The discovery of organisms that do not need oxygen suggested to Pasteur that fermentation is the equivalent of respiration carried out without oxygen: 'Fermentation is the consequence of life without air,' he said.

Yeast cells. Yeast is used to ferment wine and beer. The study of fermentation led Pasteur to his germ theory of disease.

PASTEUR AND THE END OF SPONTANEOUS GENERATION

For 2000 years people had believed that life could suddenly appear from non-living materials. This was called spontaneous generation. The Greek teacher and philosopher Aristotle (384–322BC) suggested that living things, such as frogs, snakes and insects, are constantly developing from mud, slime and other materials.

FRANCESCO REDI

In 1668 the Italian naturalist Francesco Redi disproved the theory of spontaneous generation by means of a simple but effective experiment. He placed a piece of meat in a jar covered by gauze and another piece in an uncovered jar. Because maggots appeared only in the uncovered jar, Redi concluded that they had not arisen spontaneously from the meat but had developed from eggs laid in the meat by adult flies.

MULTIPLYING MICROBES

It was still thought, however, that simple forms of life could come into being during the souring of milk, the **fermentation** of grape juice, the decay of meat and so on. In a series of experiments Pasteur demonstrated that in reality each **microbe** must be the offspring of a microbe that already exists, and that spontaneous generation does not occur. He showed that dust in the air carries microscopically small living organisms and when it settles on a suitable substance the organisms begin to multiply.

A FAMOUS EXPERIMENT

In 1860 Pasteur boiled up a meat extract to kill any **micro-organisms** that might be in it and then placed it in a flask. The flask was sealed with a bung through which ran a narrow glass tube that was bent down and then up, rather like the neck of a swan. Air could enter the flask via the tube but any particles in the air were trapped in the bottom curve of the neck. The meat broth did not spoil and no organisms appeared in it.

Milk pouring into a glass container in a dairy. Most of the milk we drink today is pasteurized to kill **bacteria**.

PASTEUR'S TRIUMPH

Pasteur presented his results at a triumphant meeting in the Sorbonne in 1864. Once and for all he had disproved the theory of spontaneous generation. Spoilage of perishable foodstuffs could be prevented by destroying the microbes already present and by protecting the **sterilized** material from future contamination.

PASTEURIZATION

That same year, 1864, Emperor Napoleon III asked Pasteur to investigate diseases that were causing considerable losses to the French wine industry. Pasteur went to a vineyard in Arbois to investigate the problem. He demonstrated that the diseases were caused by micro-organisms and that these could be killed by heating the wine to 55°Celsius for several minutes. This process, which came to be called **pasteurization**, was soon in use throughout the world to treat beer and milk as well as wine.

PASTEUR AND INFECTIOUS DISEASES

In 1865 Louis Pasteur was asked to find an answer to the diseases of silkworms that were threatening to cripple the silk industry in the south of France. He set up a laboratory in the mountains where the problem was most severe.

A moth larva of a type that is cultivated for its silk. Pasteur saved the French silk industry from disaster.

Three years of hard effort showed him that there were two diseases at work, one caused by a **parasitic protist**, the other by poor diet. He discovered how the parasites were transmitted, and how to prevent them. He worked out techniques for the selection of non-infected worms and set out other steps for the management of silkworm nurseries. This led to swift improvements in silk production and his discoveries helped to confirm his idea that each disease is caused by a specific **microbe**.

BATTLING DISEASE

From 1877 to 1887 Pasteur began to use what he had learned in the battle against infectious diseases. He began a series of studies of anthrax, a disease of farm animals that can also affect humans. Pasteur was able to show that anthrax is caused by a particular **bacillus** that can survive in the carcasses of dead animals and in soil in the form of **spores**. He fought for measures to be introduced to prevent or at least minimize the spread of disease by **micro-organisms**, and in doing so laid the ground for Joseph Lister in England to develop **antiseptic** surgery.

GIVING IMMUNITY

Pasteur observed that birds infected with old, weakened cultures of chicken cholera became resistant to infection by more dangerous forms of the disease. He produced a weakened form of the anthrax bacillus and in a dramatic experiment treated sheep and goats with the weakened organism and succeeded in giving them protection from the disease.

HONOURING JENNER

Pasteur was aware of Edward Jenner's work in the previous century and his injections of cowpox material in order to give protection against smallpox. In honour of Jenner, Pasteur suggested that the weakened cultures be called **vaccines** (from the Latin word *vacca*, meaning cow).

RABIES

In 1882 Pasteur began a study of the dreadful disease rabies. He established that it was caused by a disease agent so small that it could not be seen under the microscope. This was the first glimpse into the world of **viruses**. He developed techniques to weaken the disease agent and proved that it could then be used to vaccinate dogs against the disease.

Rabies is passed on through the bite of an infected animal. For this reason there are often strict laws about transporting animals between countries.

THE PASTEUR INSTITUTE

In 1885 he was also able to test his treatment on a human who had been bitten by a rabid dog. The patient's life was saved. Pasteur's work on rabies brought him world-wide acclaim. An international public appeal for funds financed the construction of the Pasteur Institute in 1888. In accordance with Pasteur's wishes, the Institute was founded as a clinic for rabies treatment, a research centre for infectious disease and a teaching centre. Pasteur dedicated the last seven years of his life to the Institute.

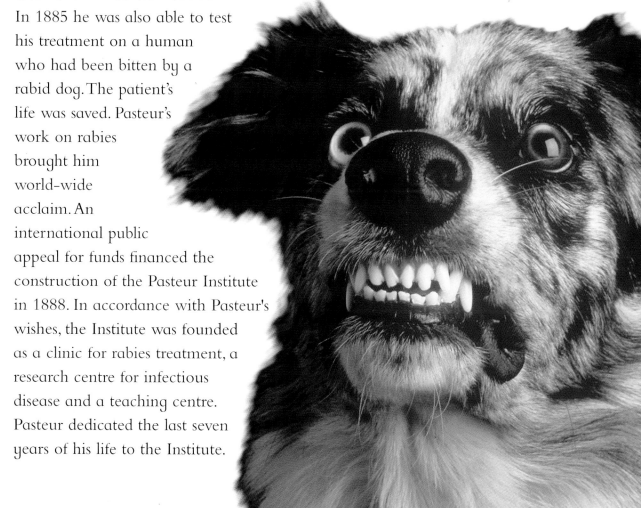

FERDINAND COHN AND THE BIRTH OF BACTERIOLOGY

Pasteur's germ theory directed the attention of other biologists to the study of the **bacteria** that were believed to be the cause of disease. One of these was the German botanist Ferdinand Cohn (1828–98). Cohn studied botany at Breslau, his birthplace in Germany, and during the early part of his career he concentrated on microscopic **algae** and **fungi** as well as other single-celled organisms. One of Cohn's great discoveries was that the internal structure of plant **cells** and animal cells is virtually the same. This was a crucial pointer to the unity of all life.

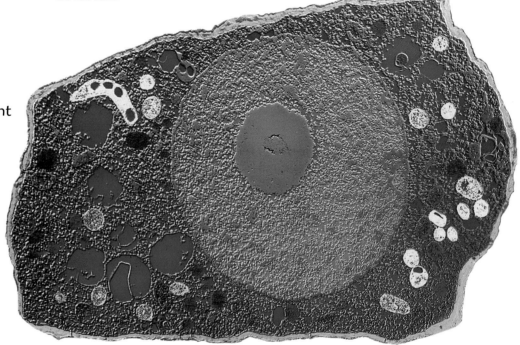

The inside of a plant cell. Cohn showed that plant and animal cells share many common features, including having a **nucleus** (shown here in red).

CLASSIFYING BACTERIA

In the 1860s Cohn turned his attention to bacteria, a subject he worked on almost exclusively for the next twenty years. In 1872 he published a three-volume work on bacteria that is often considered to be the foundation stone of the science of **bacteriology**. Cohn was the first to attempt to classify bacteria into different types and species as had been done for other living things. His system was widely accepted and today is still the basis for the modern classification of bacteria.

BACTERIAL SPORES

Cohn was the first to discover that some types of bacteria can form **spores**. A bacterial spore is a bacterium that enters a state of 'suspended animation' at times when nutrients are in short supply. All activity ceases until conditions become favourable again and the spore comes to life once more. The soil-living Clostridium bacteria, responsible for the deadly diseases of tetanus and botulism, are among those that form spores. Spores are extremely resistant to harm.

KOCH AND ANTHRAX

Shortly after Cohn's discovery of spores he was approached by Robert Koch who told him that he had unravelled the complete life history of the anthrax **bacillus**, having found that it can form spores that could lie dormant in fields for years. Cohn was impressed by Koch's work and was quick to have it published. Koch was later recognized as one of the greatest explorers of the world of bacteria.

In later years Cohn returned to his first love, the study of plants, but as a researcher in his own right and through his encouragement of others, such as Koch, he firmly established the scientific study of bacteria. He was the first to treat the study of bacteria as a separate branch of knowledge.

Anthrax spores. The *Bacillus anthracis* bacterium can remain in this form for many years, resisting heat, cold and drought.

JOSEPH LISTER AND THE BIRTH OF MODERN SURGERY

Ten years before Louis Pasteur established that **microbes** are responsible for infection and disease, Dr Ignaz Semmelweis (1818–65) in Vienna, Austria, reduced infections in women who had just given birth in hospitals by the simple but effective measure of urging doctors to wash their hands between treating each patient.

Semmelweis had noticed that the rates of infection were much higher in a maternity ward attended by medical students than in one attended by midwives. He discovered that the medical students were coming straight from examining corpses to the delivery room, and bringing infection with them. After Semmelweis required students to wash their hands the rate of infection dropped from 18 per cent to 1 per cent. Regretfully, Semmelweis' ideas about the importance of hand-washing were not accepted at the time and he died in a mental hospital.

Joseph Lister, whose introduction of antiseptic methods to the operating theatre saved countless lives.

JOSEPH LISTER

Joseph Lister (1827–1912) was born in Essex, England, and studied at the University of London. After graduating he studied medicine in London and Edinburgh, and became lecturer in surgery at Edinburgh University. Later, he became a professor of surgery and surgeon to Queen Victoria.

A drawing of the steam spray Lister used to spray a room with carbolic acid vapour.

THE IMPORTANCE OF CLEANLINESS

Even before the work of Pasteur on **fermentation** and disease agents, Lister had been convinced of the importance of scrupulous cleanliness in the operating room. Through Pasteur's work, Lister realized that the formation of pus in wounds was due to **bacteria**. Inspired by Pasteur, he reasoned that if microbes were the cause of infection, they could be killed before reaching an open wound. His method, employing carbolic acid as an **antiseptic** on dressings and instruments as well as on surgeons and patients, was a stunning success. Before the discovery of antiseptic by Lister, about 80 per cent of surgical patients contracted **gangrene**.

SAFER SURGERY

Lister's successful new procedure was soon widely accepted and adopted everywhere. Because of the great benefits it brought, Lister's work must rank as one of the great discoveries of science. It enabled millions to face surgery with far less risk than before. In 1897 he was granted the title of Baron in recognition of his work.

Robert Koch: Pioneer of Microbiology

Robert Koch (1843–1910) was born in the mining town of Clausthal in the Harz Mountains of Germany. As a boy he dreamed of being a great explorer. The world he came to explore as a man was the microscopic world of **bacteria**.

A Birthday Gift

Koch studied medicine at university and eventually became a country doctor. Always fascinated by the world around him, Koch studied small objects with his magnifying glass. On his 28th birthday his wife, Emmy, gave him a microscope. This opened up a new world for Koch to explore. He built a simple laboratory in part of his consulting room.

Anthrax

For the next three years Koch studied the deadly disease anthrax. He discovered the anthrax **bacillus** in 1876. Koch trapped a small smear of blood from an anthrax victim between two microscope slides and watched the bacteria grow and divide under his microscope. He discovered that the bacteria formed **spores** that were resistant to drying out. Koch inoculated animals with the spores and found that they developed anthrax, thus proving that the spores remained infective. This was the first time that a bacterium grown outside a living organism had been shown to cause disease. Koch published his discoveries, but they were not accepted until Pasteur demonstrated an anthrax **vaccine** in 1882.

Tracking Down Disease Agents

Koch set out to discover the disease agent that caused the dreaded disease tuberculosis. At first, he was unable to pinpoint any **micro-organisms** that might cause the disease, but in 1882 he succeeded in isolating the tubercle bacillus – the bacterium responsible. In the following year he was appointed head of a commission to study cholera in India and Egypt. In the same year he discovered the **microbe** that causes the disease.

In the early 1900s Koch went on to research tropical diseases in Africa, studying the transmission of several diseases, including sleeping sickness which he discovered was transmitted by the tsetse fly. Koch was awarded the Nobel Prize for Physiology or Medicine in 1905.

KOCH'S POSTULATES

Koch laid down a systematic method for carrying out research into identifying disease agents. The suspected agent must be identified in all of the cases examined; the agent must then be cultured through several generations; these later generations must be capable of causing the disease in a healthy animal; and the same agent must be found in the newly-infected animal as was found in the original victim. These rules, now called 'Koch's Postulates', are still largely followed today.

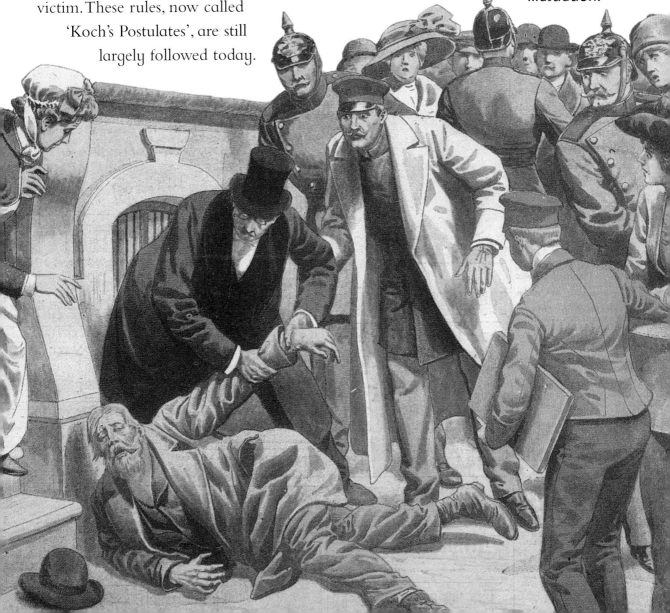

Concerned people, fearing cholera, look on as a doctor examines a man who has fallen ill in the street in this early-20th-century illustration.

PAUL EHRLICH: 'PRINCE OF SCIENCE'

Paul Ehrlich (1854–1915) was proclaimed the 'Prince of Science' during his lifetime. He grew up in a world where cholera, typhoid fever, typhus, tuberculosis and diphtheria were all feared diseases.

After university Ehrlich spent much of his early career perfecting techniques for staining the fine structure of **cells** to make them easier to examine under a microscope. One of the cell types he studied was the white blood cell, the function of which was unknown at the time.

Paul Ehrlich in his laboratory. He was the founder of chemotherapy, using chemicals to treat disease.

EHRLICH AND KOCH

In 1875 Ehrlich met Robert Koch, who is regarded as the co-founder of modern medical **bacteriology**. In 1882 Ehrlich attended a lecture Koch gave on tuberculosis and described it as one of his greatest experiences. After hearing Koch say that the tuberculosis **bacillus** was difficult to recognize, Ehrlich solved the problem within a few months by inventing a new staining technique that made it easier to identify.

ANTITOXINS

In 1891 Ehrlich joined Koch at the Institute for Infectious Diseases in Berlin. The team of scientists there included Emil Behring (1854–1917), who asked Ehrlich to help with his work on diphtheria. Researchers in Paris had discovered that diphtheria is caused by a **toxin**, or poison, produced by diphtheria bacilli and not by the bacilli themselves. Certain animals were found to be immune to the toxin, which meant that antitoxins (natural agents that acted against the toxin) might exist. The antitoxins were discovered by Behring who also realized that antitoxins from animals immunized with diphtheria toxin could be used to cure humans of the disease. Behring was awarded the first Nobel Prize for Physiology or Medicine in 1901.

ANTIBODIES

Ehrlich came up with a theory to explain the body's ability to produce antitoxins, or **antibodies**. Ehrlich thought that part of the toxin **molecule** anchored it to a 'receptor' of the cell, while a second part damaged or destroyed the cell. If the cell survived, it would produce more receptors, which eventually dropped off into the bloodstream to form antibodies. The toxins would become anchored to the antibodies rather than the cells and be made harmless.

Today we know that the human body makes antibodies in special places, such as in the glands under the arm or in the tonsils in the throat. They travel from there through the bloodstream to the infected parts of the body. Sometimes people get swollen throats or lumps in their armpits when they have infections.

A white blood cell (in blue), one of the body's defenders against infection such as the Staphylococcus bacteria (in yellow) shown here.

PHAGOCYTOSIS

The Russian biologist Elie Metchnikoff (1845–1916) discovered the process by which special white blood cells called **phagocytes** engulf **bacteria** and other foreign substances. This process is called phagocytosis. From his observations Metchnikoff concluded that phagocytosis plays a vital role in our defences against disease. Metchnikoff and Ehrlich had independently uncovered the body's main defences against disease.

Ehrlich and the Magic Bullets

Ehrlich believed that **antibodies** were like 'magic bullets' that destroyed their targets without damaging the healthy **cells** of the body. He realized that sometimes the body cannot make enough 'magic bullets' of its own. He wanted to find chemical agents that could lend a hand.

Sleeping Sickness

In 1903 British army doctor Sir David Bruce had discovered that sleeping sickness was caused by trypanosomes – **parasitic protists** that live in the blood. Ehrlich and his assistant, Kiyoshi Shiga, found that trypanosomes are sensitive to certain dyes. One of these in particular, trypan red, which Ehrlich himself had developed, had a destructive effect on the trypanosomes. There were hopes that this might lead to a cure but the results of Ehrlich's tests with trypan red were inconclusive.

Compound 606

Ehrlich believed that **compounds** containing arsenic offered the best chance of success and he and his staff prepared nearly 1000 such compounds, testing each on animals. In 1907 they reached Compound Number 606 (a chemical with the name dihydroxydiamino-arsenobenzene hydrochloride). This proved ineffective against trypanosomes and so was filed away and ignored.

However, Compound 606 was investigated again in 1909 and found to be effective against spirochaetes, the parasites that cause the disease syphilis, which can lead to blindness, insanity and death. Ehrlich tried the compound on himself, without any harm, and in 1910 announced the discovery of the chemical, now called Salvarsan, as a treatment for syphilis. Ehrlich had found his first magic bullet.

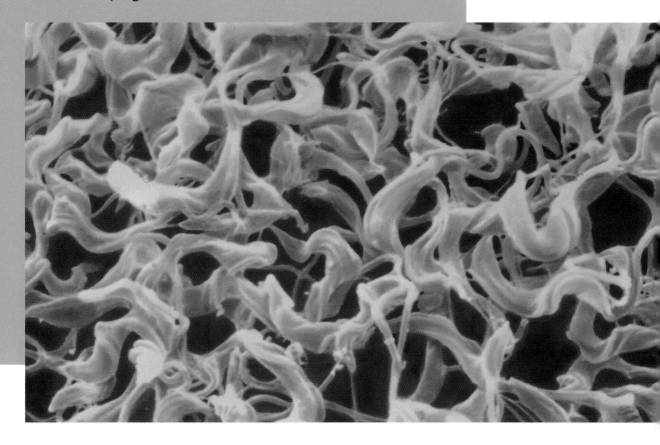

A tangle of trypanosomes, the protistan parasites that are the cause of sleeping sickness.

CHEMOTHERAPY

Doctors and the public hailed the discovery of this treatment for syphilis. In cities such as Paris and Berlin, syphilis affected up to 10 per cent of the population. By the end of 1910 around 30,000 patients had been treated. Ehrlich had founded modern **chemotherapy**, a word he himself used for the first time.

Ehrlich received many honours in the course of his life, including the Nobel Prize for Physiology or Medicine in 1908 (shared with Elie Metchnikoff) for his services to medical research and his work on the body's immune system. When he died in 1915 the London *Times* newspaper said that he had 'opened new doors to the unknown'.

ALEXANDER FLEMING AND ANTIBIOTICS

Alexander Fleming (1881–1955), the son of a farmer, was born in Ayrshire, Scotland. He won a scholarship to study medicine at St Mary's Hospital Medical School, London, in 1902. After his graduation he stayed in the hospital's **bacteriology** department and worked there for the rest of his career.

LYSOZYME

During the First World War Fleming began searching for antibacterial substances. In 1922 he discovered lysozyme, an **enzyme** that attacks many types of **bacteria**. Lysozyme is found in nasal mucus, tears and saliva, where it is involved in killing bacteria by breaking down the **carbohydrates** surrounding them. Fleming later showed it to be present in most body fluids and tissues. Lysozyme has become a useful research tool and is used for dissolving bacteria for chemical examination.

DISCOVERY OF PENICILLIN

Fleming made the discovery for which he is famous by accident. In 1928 he was working with the bacterium *Staphylococcus aureus*. One day he noticed that specks of green mould had appeared on one of the dishes that a bacterial colony was growing on. The bacteria around the specks had disappeared.

Alexander Fleming, the discoverer of antibiotics, at work in his laboratory.

Fleming took some of the mould and found that it formed a felt-like layer on the surface of the nutrient broth he grew it on. He filtered this layer off and tested it on a range of bacteria. Some of the disease bacteria were killed by the mould. Fleming was able to identify the mould as *Penicillium notatum*, a species related to the mould that grows on stale bread. He called the antibacterial substance it produced 'penicillin'.

FLOREY AND CHAIN

Purifying and concentrating penicillin from the mould was a problem for a chemist to solve and Fleming was not a chemist. Australian chemist Howard Florey had come to London in the late 1930s where he had worked on lysozyme for a while before becoming interested in penicillin. Florey, together with German scientist Ernst Chain, succeeded in extracting penicillin and developing it into an **antibiotic** that could be used in medicine. Fleming, Florey and Chain shared the 1945 Nobel Prize in Physiology or Medicine.

A NEW WONDER DRUG

The first person to be treated with penicillin was a policeman dying of blood poisoning. Unfortunately there was not enough penicillin to stop the growth of the bacteria that were poisoning his blood. Although he got better for a short time he became ill again and died. However, Florey had now proved that bacterial infections could be successfully treated with penicillin. He went to the United States where he persuaded drug companies to grow Penicillium mould. Large amounts of penicillin were produced. During the Second World War thousands of lives were saved by the new wonder drug.

Penicillin, the first of the antibiotics, has been used with great success in the treatment of many bacterial diseases, including pneumonia, scarlet fever and meningitis.

MARTINUS BEIJERINCK AND THE DISCOVERY OF VIRUSES

Louis Pasteur had guessed that there might be disease agents too small to be visible under the microscope. For example, he had never found the agent responsible for rabies.

TOBACCO MOSAIC

In 1892 Dmitry Ivanovsky (1864–1920), a Russian botanist, investigated the **sap** from tobacco plants affected by mosaic disease. This is a condition that stunts the growth of tobacco plants and mottles their leaves in a characteristic mosaic pattern. He passed the sap through filters so fine that they would trap all known **bacteria**. Yet the sap still retained its ability to produce the disease in new plants. Ivanovsky did not fully grasp the implications of his discovery. He still believed the disease to be caused by bacteria and thought that there was a flaw in his filter.

BEIJERINCK

Martinus Willem Beijerinck (1851–1931) was born in Amsterdam. His earliest scientific interest was botany, which he taught to provide himself with an income while studying for his doctorate, which he obtained in 1877.

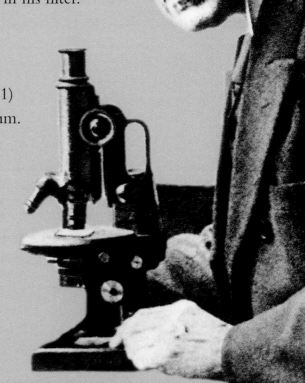

A LOVE OF BACTERIA

In the early 1880s Beijerinck began studying tobacco mosaic. His search for a bacterium that caused the disease was in vain. However, the work awakened an interest in bacteria. Beijerinck took a job as a **bacteriologist** with an industrial company and set about learning all he could about the subject. One of his most significant achievements was identifying the bacteria that live in **nodules** on the roots of plants such as peas and beans and perform the important task of converting atmospheric nitrogen into **compounds** necessary for the plant's growth.

LIQUID POISON

In 1895 Beijerinck returned to an academic career in Delft. Here he resumed his study of tobacco mosaic and once more tried to identify the disease agent responsible. He pressed out the juice of infected tobacco leaves and found, as Ivanovsky had, that the juice alone was able to infect healthy plants. However, he could find no trace of bacteria in the juice and nothing would grow from it on his culture dishes. Like Ivanovsky, he found that the juice infected a healthy plant even after filtering.

Later, Beijerinck discovered that he could infect a healthy plant and from that plant infect another healthy plant, and so on for as long as he cared to continue. This meant that the disease agent must be capable of reproducing itself. If it was just a liquid poison its effects would weaken and disappear. However, he believed that the liquid itself was alive, calling it a 'filterable **virus**', from the Latin word for poison. It would be another forty years before Wendell Stanley began to uncover the true nature of viruses.

Martinus Beijerinck (left), who was the first to discover the existence of viruses.

Tobacco mosaic virus particles. The viral **genetic** material is protected within a tightly wound **protein helix**.

WENDELL STANLEY AND THE CRYSTAL INVADERS

During the three decades following Beijerinck's findings, many more 'filterable **viruses**' were discovered. Viruses were found in animals, plants, insects and even **bacteria**. Unlike other microscopic disease agents, however, the mysterious viruses proved impossible to grow in the absence of the **cells** they attacked. In the 1930s a number of new techniques were developed for the study of viruses, called virology.

WENDELL STANLEY

One man who was at the forefront of these developments was Wendell Stanley (1904–71), an American **biochemist**. After he obtained his doctorate he was working at the Rockefeller Institute for Medical Research in the 1930s. Like Beijerinck and Ivanovsky before him, he turned to the study of tobacco mosaic.

CRYSTAL VIRUSES

Stanley set about growing large numbers of plants and infecting them. He planned to use a technique developed by chemists to form **crystals** from **proteins** because he believed that a virus was a protein **molecule**. He mashed up leaves from his infected plants and carried out the procedure. In 1935 he succeeded in obtaining a number of fine, needle-like crystals. By themselves they were harmless, but as soon as a solution of the crystals was introduced into a healthy plant they had all the infective properties of the virus.

NUCLEIC ACIDS AT THE HEART OF LIFE

This was a puzzle. How could something that appeared to be living become an apparently non-living crystal? The virus, it seemed, straddled the shadowy boundary between the living and non-living worlds. The answer lay within it. In 1937 Sir Frederick Bawden succeeded in showing that the mosaic virus contained **RNA**, one of the **nucleic acids**. Nucleic acids, either RNA or **DNA**, are found in all viruses, and indeed in all forms of life. In fact, the presence of nucleic acids may be the most basic requirement for life.

THE SECRETS OF HEREDITY

It was the study of viruses and bacteria that pointed scientists in the direction of nucleic acids as the carriers of **genetic** information. The path to this discovery is followed on the next page.

A computer graphic of the long-chain protein molecules that make up one side of the 12-sided carnation mottle virus. Genetically, this is one of the simplest viruses and it is often used in virus research.

Oswald Avery and the Search for Heredity

In the 1860s the Swiss **biochemist** Friedrich Miescher (1844–95) carried out the first carefully planned chemical studies of the **nuclei** of **cells**. Miescher detected a substance in the nucleus that he named nuclein. This contained an acidic component. Two main types of these nucleic acids were identified: ribonucleic acid (**RNA**) and deoxyribonucleic acid (**DNA**). Their function in the cell remained a mystery.

Nucleic Acid and Inheritance

Miescher and others suspected that nuclein or **nucleic acid** might play a key role in **heredity**, but others argued that they appeared to be too simple chemically to carry such complex information. It was not until 1943 that the first direct evidence emerged that pointed towards DNA as the carrier of **genetic** information.

Oswald Avery

Oswald Theodore Avery (1877–1955) was born in Halifax, Nova Scotia, but spent most of his life in New York City. After qualifying in medicine in 1904 at Columbia University, he spent a brief period as a clinical physician, but soon turned to research in **bacteriology** and **immunology**. In 1913 he joined the Rockefeller Institute Hospital in New York, where he worked until his retirement in 1948. Avery's most important work concerned transformation – a process by which the characteristics of one species of **bacterium** are incorporated into another species.

The Transforming Agent

In 1928 British bacteriologist Fred Griffith reported that he had injected mice with a mixture of two strains of the same pneumonia-causing bacterium, one potentially lethal but dead, the other living but harmless. Despite the fact that each of the mixture's components was harmless, the mice contracted pneumonia. Griffith was able to isolate virulent, living bacteria from the dead mice. He proposed that some agent from the dead bacteria had somehow transformed the harmless living bacteria and made them deadly. Furthermore, when the living bacteria reproduced, the offspring were deadly too. This suggested that the transforming agent had been incorporated into the bacteria's genes.

DNA – THE MOLECULE OF HEREDITY

Avery and his colleagues Colin MacLeod and Maclyn McCarthy began investigating the nature of the transforming agent. In 1943 they obtained a pure sample of a virulent, living bacterium and killed it by heat treatment. The bacteria's DNA was extracted and added to a living, harmless strain of the bacterium. The offspring of these bacteria were found to be disease-causing. Avery had proved that the transforming agent was DNA. Other researchers soon established that DNA was the **molecule** of heredity.

Oswald Avery, whose work pointed towards DNA being the carrier of hereditary information in the cell.

In 1952 Alfred Hershey and Martha Chase showed that when a bacteriophage (a **virus** that attacks a bacterium) infects its host, it is the DNA of the virus, and not its **protein** coat, that enters the host cell and provides the information needed for the virus to be reproduced in the cell.

WATSON AND CRICK: UNRAVELLING THE HELIX

The experiments of Avery and his colleagues, and Hershey and Chase, had made it plain that **DNA** was the carrier of **genetic** information in all living **cells**. The mystery that now had to be solved was how DNA carried and transmitted this information.

A RECIPE FOR DNA

Chemical studies had already shown that DNA is made up of a number of repeating subunits, called nucleotides. Each nucleotide has one of four different structures called bases: adenine (A) and guanine (G), together with thymine (T) and cytosine (C). A vital clue to the way DNA works was uncovered by Erwin Chargaff at Columbia University in the late 1940s. He found that the number of As is always equal to the number of Ts; and the number of Gs always matches the number of Cs. These were important pointers to the structure of DNA, and the way genetic information is coded.

A simple representation of part of a DNA molecule showing how the nucleotides always link in the same pairings.

ROSALIND FRANKLIN

DNA is much too small to be seen through the microscope so other techniques had to be used to gather information on its structure. One of these was X-ray crystallography. This involved using X-rays to take shadowy 'pictures' of the DNA **molecule**. One of the foremost crystallographers was Rosalind Franklin (1920–58) at King's College, London. In 1951 she gave a lecture on her findings in which she tentatively suggested that the DNA molecule was a 'big **helix**'.

ENTER WATSON AND CRICK

Franklin's talk was attended by James Watson, an American geneticist. Together with Francis Crick, a British physicist, he was trying to piece together all the clues to the structure of DNA. Watson and Crick met in the autumn of 1951 when Watson arrived at the Cavendish Laboratory in Cambridge, England. Watson was a child prodigy from Chicago who had earned his PhD in genetics from Indiana University at the age of 22. Crick, twelve years older than Watson, was still pursuing his doctorate in the X-ray studies of **proteins**. Both were committed to unravelling the DNA mystery and they soon formed a partnership.

An X-ray crystallography image of DNA. It takes great skill to 'read' one of these images. The circle around the outside is caused by water in the crystal, not by the DNA.

PIECES OF THE PUZZLE

They were taking information from the findings of other scientists and trying to bring it all together like the pieces of a jigsaw puzzle. Solving the puzzle meant incorporating the findings of Chargaff with those of Franklin. Carelessly, Watson took no notes at Franklin's talk and when he returned to Crick at the Cavendish Laboratory in Cambridge he misremembered important parts of what he had heard. The result was that Watson and Crick built a DNA model that was quite wrong, as Franklin was quick to tell them when she saw it. Sir Lawrence Bragg, head of the Cavendish Laboratory, ordered Watson and Crick to leave DNA to the King's College researchers.

WATSON AND CRICK: MOLECULE MODEL-MAKING

Throughout 1952 Francis Crick concentrated on his doctorate and James Watson studied the mating of **bacteria**. In January 1953 their interest in **DNA** was sparked once more when Linus Pauling (1901–94), one of the world's foremost chemists, published a proposed structure for DNA. Pauling's model turned out to be inaccurate but Watson and Crick were determined to return to their efforts and crack the problem before Pauling, or anyone else, did.

MAURICE WILKINS

They knew that Rosalind Franklin's X-ray pictures were crucial to finding the solution. Watson travelled to King's College where he met Maurice Wilkins. Franklin and Wilkins were supposedly working together, but Wilkins treated Franklin like an assistant rather than as a researcher in her own right. Franklin objected strongly to this and refused to share her findings with Wilkins if he could not treat her as an equal. Wilkins revealed to Watson that he had been secretly copying Franklin's findings and showed Watson one of her DNA X-ray pictures. Watson realized that it confirmed that DNA was a **helix**.

THE DOUBLE-HELIX REVEALED

Back at the Cavendish, Watson and Crick concentrated on building a DNA model. The object was to order the atoms within the **molecule** in a way that fitted everything that was known about its composition and also provide a mechanism for the molecule to replicate itself accurately. By 7 March 1953, after much trial and error, they had the answer. DNA is a double-helix, two strands twined around each other with the bases paired up across the centre. As Chargaff's findings had predicted, A always paired with T, and G with C. This is called the 'complementary pairing' of the four bases in each DNA strand.

MESELSON AND STAHL

In 1958 American scientists Matthew Meselson and Franklin Stahl showed that when a **cell** divides, half of the original DNA ends up in one cell and half in the other. The two strands of the original DNA molecule separate and each of the old strands is used as a template to build a new one. Because the bases are always paired in the same way, exact copies of the original DNA are formed.

James Watson (left) and Francis Crick (right) with the model of the DNA molecule that they constructed in the Cavendish Laboratory.

PRIZE WINNERS

Sadly, Rosalind Franklin died of cancer in 1958 at the early age of 37. Had she lived, she might have shared the Nobel Prize with Watson and Crick in 1962. The Nobel Prize, however, is only awarded to living scientists. Watson and Crick shared the prize with Maurice Wilkins, who was credited with Franklin's DNA work as well as his own.

Stanley Prusiner's Prions

In 1972 American medic Stanley Prusiner (1942–) had a patient who died of dementia resulting from Creutzfeldt-Jakob disease (CJD). CJD turns the brain into a spongelike mass, resulting in an inability to walk properly, uncontrollable movements of the limbs, distorted speech and eventual death. CJD is estimated to affect about one in a million people worldwide. A similar disease, bovine spongiform encephalitis, or BSE, was known to affect cattle while a disease called scrapie affected sheep. It was believed that CJD, BSE and scrapie might have the same cause.

Taking Up The Challenge

Prusiner decided to take up the challenge of identifying the disease agent that was the cause of CJD. In 1982, after ten years of effort, he and his colleagues successfully produced a preparation that contained a single infectious agent. All the experimental evidence they had before them seemed to indicate that the disease agent was a single **protein**. Prusiner named the agent a **prion**, a name he derived from 'proteinaceous infectious particle'. This was a startling idea, since all known disease agents, and indeed all forms of life, contained **hereditary** material in the form of **DNA** or **RNA**. His discovery was met with disbelief by other scientists. Prusiner continued to try to pin down the exact nature of this strange new disease agent.

A researcher into BSE holds a jar containing the brain of a cow that was killed by the disease.

Prions Everywhere

Every protein is coded by a **gene**, a segment of DNA or RNA. So where was the gene for the prion? Was the actual disease agent an undiscovered **virus** that carried the code for the prion within its genetic material?

In 1984 Prusiner and his colleagues showed, astonishingly, that the prion gene was to be found in every mammal they tested, including humans. This raised the question of why something that was found in all mammals could in some cases prove to be so deadly. What was the trigger?

CHAIN REACTION

Prusiner's next discovery was that the prion protein came in two distinct shapes, one normal and harmless and one that resulted in disease. The disease-causing prion could trigger a chain reaction in which the normal protein is flipped into the disease form. Over time, which could be months to years, the disease-causing form can reach levels that result in brain damage.

KNOCK-OUT MICE

Prusiner demonstrated that the normal prion protein was an ordinary component of white blood **cells** and was found in many other tissues as well. Normal prion proteins are found in particularly large numbers on the surface of nerve cells in the brain.

In 1992 researchers succeeded in removing the gene that codes for the prion protein in mice, creating 'prion knock-out mice'. These prion knock-out mice were completely resistant to infection when exposed to disease-causing prions. Strangely, the prion knock-out mice appeared healthy, which suggests that the prion protein is not essential. What its role in the body might be has yet to be determined.

In 1997 Stanley Prusiner was awarded the Nobel Prize in Physiology or Medicine for his 'pioneering discovery of an entirely new genre of disease-causing agents'.

Prion fibrils (in orange) in the brain of a cow infected with BSE. These fibrils are thought to be collections of the prion protein that causes the disease.

GLOSSARY

alga(e) non-flowering single-celled plant, usually living in water

antibiotic substance produced by or obtained from certain bacteria or fungi that can be used to kill or inhibit the growth of disease-causing micro-organisms

antibody defensive protein produced by an organism in response to the presence of foreign or invading substances such as the proteins found on viruses or bacteria

antiseptic preventing the growth of disease-causing micro-organisms

bacillus a rod shaped bacterium

bacteriology study of bacteria

bacterium (plural bacteria) any of a large group of single-celled organisms which have no organized nucleus

biochemistry study of chemical processes in living things

carbohydrate one of a group of energy-producing compounds containing carbon, hydrogen and oxygen, such as glucose and other sugars

catalyst substance that alters the rate of a chemical reaction without undergoing any permanent change itself

cell the basic unit of life. Cells can exist as independent life forms, such as bacteria and protists, or form tissues in more complicated life forms, such as muscle cells and nerve cells in animals.

chemotherapy treatment of disease using chemicals. Chemotherapy is commonly used in the treatment of cancer.

compound in chemistry, a substance combining two or more elements

crystal solid in which the atoms or molecules are arranged in an orderly way, giving it a surface with well-defined smooth faces

DNA (deoxyribonucleic acid) genetic material of almost all living things with the exception of some viruses. DNA consists of two long chains of nucleotides joined together in a double helix.

enzyme type of protein produced in a living thing that acts as a catalyst in a chemical reaction

ethics rules or principles that tell us what is right and what is wrong

faculty part of a university, usually including a specific subject area

ferment chemical breakdown of sugars using bacteria or yeasts. Fermentation is used in baking bread, making wine and beer, producing cheese and in other food production.

fungus any of a group of spore-producing organisms that includes mushrooms and moulds

gangrene death or decomposition of part of the body tissue, often due to bacterial infection

gene unit of heredity. A gene is a length of DNA and a number of genes are carried on a chromosome. A gene is a set of instructions for assembling a protein from amino acids.

helix corkscrew-shaped curve. The double-helix of DNA is made up of two of these entwined with each other.

heredity genetic passing on of characteristics from one generation to the next

immunology study of immunity and the body's immune system

microbe micro-organism

micro-organism any microscopic living thing, such as bacteria and protists

molecule group of atoms. A molecule is the smallest part of a compound that can take part in a chemical reaction.

nodule small swelling or build-up of cells

nucleic acid DNA and RNA. DNA encodes genetic information and RNA 'reads' this information and translates it into protein production.

nucleus dense centre of a eukaryote cell that contains the genetic material

optics science of light, including the use of lenses in instruments such as microscopes

parasite one organism living on another and benefiting without giving anything in return

pasteurize sterilize by heating

phagocyte type of cell capable of absorbing foreign matter, especially bacteria

prion protein particle believed to be the cause of diseases such as BSE and scrapie

protein one of a group of complex organic molecules that perform a variety of essential tasks in living things, including providing structure and controlling the rates of chemical reactions

protist any single-celled eukaryote organism of the kingdom Protista such as algae

RNA (ribonucleic acid) found in different forms within cells, RNA is involved in the process by which the genetic code of DNA is translated into the production of proteins in the cell

sap fluid circulating in plants that carries nutrients and water to the plant tissues

spore resting or dormant state of a bacterium, entered when conditions are unfavourable. A spore can resist hostile conditions for long periods of time.

sterilize clean thoroughly, free from micro-organisms

toxin poisonous substance produced by an organism such as a bacterium

vaccination inoculate using a vaccine to give immunity against a particular disease

virus infective particle, usually consisting of a molecule of nucleic acid

INDEX